D1307700

Signature Planner Journals
www.signatureplannerjournals.com
www.signatureplannerjournals.co.uk

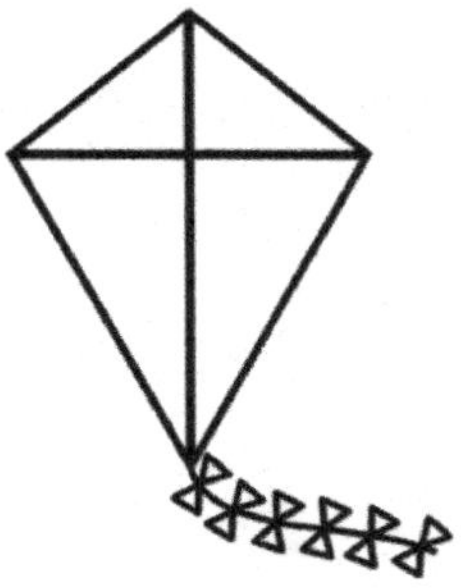

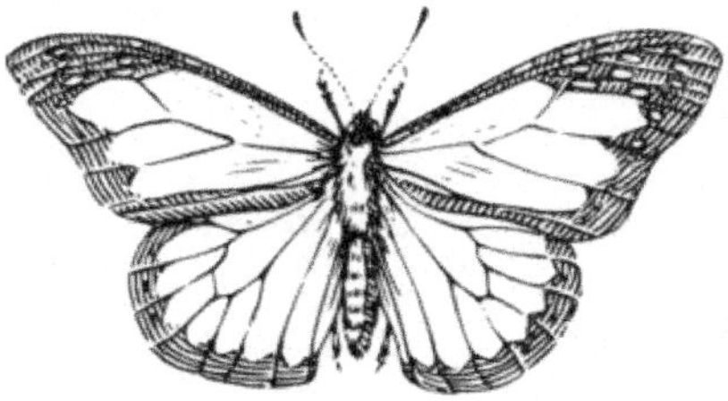

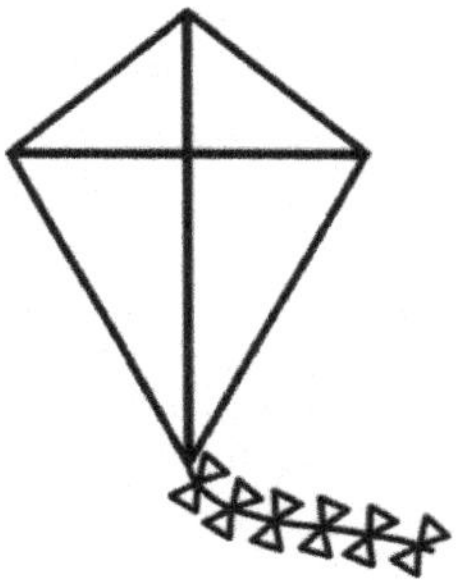

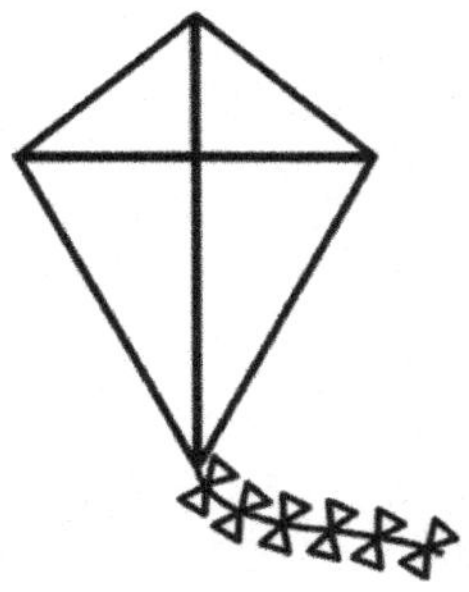

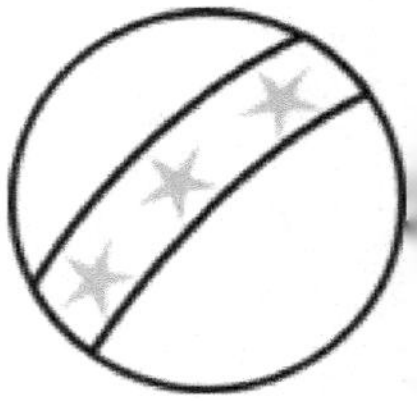

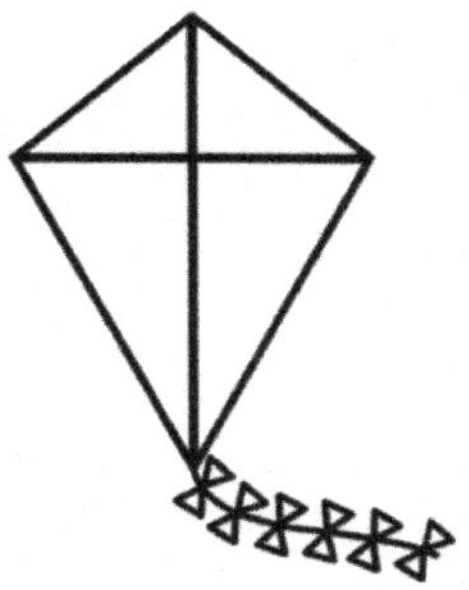

27019953R00046

Made in the USA
Middletown, DE
19 December 2018